The Tablet

_____

_____

Open Task

Published by OpenTask, Republic of Ireland

Notebook design © 2013 by Dmitry Vostokov

OpenTask notebooks are available through booksellers and
distributors worldwide. For further information or comments send
requests to press@opentask.com.

ISBN-13: 978-1-908043-55-9 (Paperback)
Version 1.0, 2013